"Damn, this book is good. Matt Miller's writing brings to mind
Richard Sennett's treatise on the joys and value of making,
The Craftsman, wherein he celebrates discipline, commitment, and the
time it takes to produce quality work. It also evokes Donald Hall's
famous essay, 'Poetry and Ambition,' in which he laments the
lack of such seriousness among contemporary poets and the advent of
what he calls the 'McPoem'—cobbled quickly, shabbily,
and with very little ambition toward memorability.
I believe that both Sennett and Hall would agree with me
that Matt Miller is a craftsman of the first order.
And his most recent collection, *Tender the River*,
is well-wrought, exquisite, and built to last.
Beautiful as a bespoke three-piece,
useful as a pair of hand-crafted brogues."

—John Murillo, author of *Kontemporary Amerikan Poetry*

D1217878

TENDER THE RIVER

Tender the River

POEMS

MATT W. MILLER

Texas Review Press • Huntsville, Texas

Published by Texas Review Press
Huntsville, Texas 77341

Library of Congress Cataloging-in-Publication Data

Names: Miller, Matt W., 1973– author.
Title: Tender the river : poems / by Matt W. Miller.
Description: Huntsville, Texas : Texas Review Press, [2021]
Identifiers: LCCN 2020041581 (print) | LCCN 2020041582 (ebook) | ISBN 9781680032246
    (paperback) | ISBN 9781680032253 (ebook)
Subjects: LCSH: Merrimack River (N.H. and Mass.)—Poetry. | LCGFT: Ecopoetry. |
    Autobiographical poetry.
Classification: LCC PS3613.I54525 T46 2021 (print) | LCC PS3613.I54525 (ebook) |
    DDC 811/.6—dc23
LC record available at https://lccn.loc.gov/2020041581
LC ebook record available at https://lccn.loc.gov/2020041582

Cover photo courtesy Mike Weinhold, *Lowell Textile Mills*, ©2016.

for the people of Lowell, for all of those living and loving,
laughing and surviving, along the Merrimack River,
forever the source, forever the waters rolling on,
forever the song

CONTENTS

by Andre Dubus III

All of my blood relatives, including my mother and late father, were raised in Louisiana, but I have lived in the Merrimack Valley since I was a boy. We migrated here for my father's job, but after a ten-year marriage my parents divorced, and I and my siblings moved with our single mother from one cheap rented house to another along the Merrimack River, a living, breathing serpent of history that Matt Miller renders so gloriously in this mesmerizing new collection.

In three of these truly remarkable poems, Miller writes from the point of view of the river itself: "Some days, so filled with rage and rain, / I rip this whole town down . . . / . . . my whitewater wall / showing you just how ugly pretty I can call out // all the beat and broken ways you bit my dirt / with hammer and shovel, with reeking load/ of angles and invention."

"Rage and rain," "ugly pretty," "beat and broken ways." This gritty, expressionistic language reflects perfectly my own subjective memory not only of the river itself but of these half-dead mill towns on its muddy banks, places I have lived in and around for most of my life. But unlike Matt Miller, I am not a native of this part of the world. And so, even after over fifty years of living in this river valley, and even after raising our three children here at the mouth of the Merrimack River, I still feel like an outsider. One of the many strengths of *Tender the River*, however, is that it is clearly written from the point of view of a deep insider, one who was raised by his extended family in the largest textile town on the river, Lowell, Massachusetts.

Many of these extraordinary poems are of Miller's own childhood: from skateboarding along Lowell's broken sidewalks and streets; to playing Little League games with a kid who later got a machete swung into his skull; to being on the high school football team in the shadow of a legendary grandfather; to driving an old Buick through the potholed lot where a Cambodian boy, a quiet classmate, was shot to death for trying to leave a gang; to the flash of violence between boys who do not even know one another, the plaintive refrain "we did nothing to make those kids hate us"; to Miller losing his father in the same hospital where "he watched us being born."

But as intimate and moving as these poems are, the scope of *Tender the River* is truly epic, capturing the sweep of this river valley's history from its geological birth during the Ice Age to it being the natural home of its "first tribes," who named the water "Merroh Awke" (Strong Place). Miller then takes us through the Industrial Revolution and all the girls and women who worked in the mills—"your cradle / of fly wheel, of factory, your mill / girl offering, your doffers, your biddies, your boom / and your busted," the unrelenting "schika tak schika taka schika tak" of the looms; to the mills going dark and the rise of heroin and Oxycontin and gangs; to Lowell's ten police stations and "bars / and bars and bars, one for every St. Anne's, / Immaculate, and St. Patrick's."

Savoring these thirty-eight deeply evocative and compelling poems feels like being in a sustained trance cast by a master novelist, the cumulative power of the narrative here unmistakable. Yet the ambitious depth and breadth of Miller's new work is only part of what is so successful; and while I am a prose writer and not a poet, I cannot get over the stylistic prowess of the language displayed in each and every poem. Whether Miller is writing about having been a boy in the alleyways along those old canals, or being a woman working a loom for hours on end, or being the river itself, his verse is as free-wheeling yet restrained as a jazz trumpet in the exquisitely sure hands of Miles Davis. In "Said the River When I Begged for His Song," Miller writes:

And now you come sucking up for a song,
now you're kneeling and begging for my breath,
mumbling how you're so humbled in my mud,
making me your messed-up amalgam of mother
and lover, professing some mission to recover
the missing past and plasma of your blood.

But that is just what Matt W. Miller achieves in this, his finest book yet, a deep recovery not just of his missing "past and plasma" but of ours as well. For that is what art of this caliber does; it takes us through darkness and shadow to the kind of light that can only come from truth and beauty and the clear love that Miller still holds for these worn cobbled streets along this ancient but still flowing river.

A drop of water, if it could write out its own history,
would explain the universe to us.

—*Lucy Larcom*

Autobiography

For a moment I was a failed skip of stone
sunk into the river for a moment I was the river
purling in long last shadows of September
for a moment I was a skinny grizzly spitting
into a beer can for a time I was Christmas
lights wrapping around downtown's smokestack
until I became a book filled with baby teeth
for a while I was a boy painting the portrait
of a queen for a while I was a child queen
for a while I knew the switches to every light
knew the angles of every kiss in the autumn
night and shaped morning from the curve
of her hips for a while I spelled the difference
between church and lips for a while I was
young for a while I was son for a while I
was father of a million reasons not to pray
for a while god begged me for apology
for a while I was an apology walking the edge
of the dam for a while I was dust on the floor
of a cotton mill swept by a broom out into
summer for a while I was summer until liver
spotted clouds blew over the dunes to fling
the monarchs into Mexico for a while I was
oyamel fir and yucca tree after all sap ran
desert west after sugar maple elm and pine
for a moment there I had made up my mind
to be worm for the plover for a second I
believed I was enough vessel for my children
for a night my wife was able to rest on our blade
of stars for one moon the sea could trade us
for the sun for one dawn we filched the horizon

I

I know water is my ink, memory my blood

—*Arthur Sze*

Invocation at the Merrimack

And now I take a tongue into your mud,
into your syringe and soda bottle banks,

to beg your braided silk, your Pennacook
ikwe, your sliding tar of snake, your mouth
of stones, your clavicle

                 of roil and moan,
your lover ghosts thrown from Pawtucket Falls,
your whitewater of bread and roses,

                   your creak
of locks and lifts, your leap from burning windows,

your fished-out crib of salmon and shiv, of shell
casings and shad, alewife and boosted tires,
your cradle

             of flywheel, of factory, your mill
girl offering, your doffers, your biddies, your boom

and your busted. Penitent palmed I stand
in this, your sun tussling dawn, to call a song.

My river, roll your blueblack big hips under
the oxidized iron of cantilever and cable,

deluge and slip bridge ribs and sing between
the redbrick and brackish heft of textile mills
turned art galleries with crack alleys.

You,
bender of flashboard pins, come

                        sing to me,
sluice me, double back and seduce me to

your flood, tenor me down to your Irish blood
canals, your Greek restaurant ghettos,
fluorescent Cambodian groceries, chunk heeled
Brazilian bakeries,

                  your cobblestones
exposed to sell some rheumy history.

Bones old and broken of flesh, in sack and ash,
I call a song.

                  You ferried me home, now drink
and spit me out where city hall has crouched
inside downtown's diverticula,

down to the fountain at JFK plaza where
my brother was suckered by a kid I wouldn't
hit back.

            And there, just one of ten police stations,
Pollard library, and across Arcand Ave,
Lowell High, its field house named after
our grandfather,

                 the columned Masonic temple,
the bring your own wine Viet Thai, and bars
and bars and bars, one for every St. Anne's,
Immaculate, and St. Patrick's.

                        In your
hydraulic drop prayers are tossed like toasts
to tilted pints. There, here, my palms unfold.

                 Give willow to me against
my flooded nights, against my broken rites.

So you flow down and roll stones old river,
and moor me here for what I am and not.

Wake my song and pluck me to your pulse.
I'll stay down in your valley,
                        drink your ink
of water and dream myself

                        back into you.

Make me small again, roll me in your lap,
your mud, your moon lit blood.

                 Supplicated,
by the greasy vents of a train car diner, I beg
your lip of water
                        to whisper.

Boys Beyond June

My brother and I played Little League
with Marcus and oh shit that kid could hit
and just lights out at short I mean
he balled and ran as mad as winter
rivers so when ten years later
he walks into the packy where
we're buying bourbon and a sleeve
of dip and see the staples holding
together his cornrowed skull we ask
him and he laughs saying the dude
of this girl that he was banging whacked
him from behind with a machete
when he was walking out of a house
party and from the way he tells
us Marcus seems to feel that this
was the worst part like a move like that
was rude or something like to jump
out from the bushes behind porch steps
was *straight up punk and now the part*
in my hair is forever fucked he says
and then he pays for his case of Beast
then we all bullshit our see-you-soons
and my brother and I walk out the door
onto the busted concrete lot
across from the autobody shop
and see the lights leaking out
from miniblinds of multifamily
homes lining Concord Street
and we shake our heads and try to laugh
the way that Marcus always laughed

staring down Brad Pacheco pitching
him chin music with bases jacked
and all the dust the sudden dusk
and all our summer ahead of us

Ghazal: Augumtoocooke

North side of the Merrimack is what the Pennacook called Augumtoocooke,
but as I drive east along Pawtucket Boulevard there's no seeing Augumtoocooke.

That road pours into Varnum Ave then onto the VFW Highway so on my left I
see
Heritage Park, the University, a Mickey D's, Dad's frat, but not Augumtoocooke.

The Pawtucket Falls lap lazy over the wooden flashings of a dam built to max out
the river's hydraulic head and where once fished first people of the
Augumtoocooke.

Across the river, Fox Hall Towers, tallest building here to Boston, Lelacheur
Park,
Tsongas Arena, ribbons of redbrick mills, all that looks down over
Agumtoocooke.

Bang a larry at the lights on Bridge Street, roll past Little Caesars, Manning
Liquor,
watch landscaping crews smoke morning butts by a Dunks, but no
Augumtoocooke.

Down by Macpherson Park, lithe Irish, Cambodian, Greek, and Dominican boys
sweat half-court hoops brilliant under the rim knowing shit about
Augumtoocooke,

though it might get a mention at McAuliffe Elementary studying Indians a whole
week
before Thanksgiving break, before Christmas snow blows in to bury
Augumtoocooke.

Now I roll into what's left of Dracut, bought for four yards of duffel and a pound
of tobacco from the daughter of the sachem who hunted the marshes of
　　Augumtoocooke.

There's no more game in the marshes. There're no more marshes. But at night,
　　the reservoir
was a good teenage spot to drop boomers and think, *Wow, I am sooo about*
　　Augumtoocooke,

so deep in breezes of some better yesterday and if only I could strip me down into that way
of life I'd be so pure, so alive diving into Beaver Brook under the moon of
　　Augumtoocooke!

Driving a busted-out Chevy, missing all I see to arrogate the used-to-be, dream-
　　ing absolution
from history, from my millboy misery, I seek a cradle in the crook of
　　Augumtoocooke.

Such bullshit. Nothing but what I took, what I take and take, what I break to
　　make my egg
bob in some unpoisoned pond where I can drop a line, some kind of
　　Augumtoocooke

of my mind. But it's not mine. It's a land apart, outside time, and ever our
　　infinite theft
milled from the sagging pines of this Augumtoocooke, Augumtoocooke,
　　Augumtoocooke.

Eve, Bumming a Smoke on a Porch in Pawtucketville

The female is, as it were, a deformed male, and the catamenia are semen, only not pure; for there is only one thing they have not in them, the principle of soul.
— Aristotle

I'm told I'm born from crooked bone

       that I arrived ready to break they say I am

mutilated man that I am not but that which

       provides base matter that I am neither sculptor

maker nor creator that I am seduced transgressor

       selfish lover that I am moon polluted and pierced

with serpent's arrow that I am the fertile field

       to harrow that I am an apology that has yet to happen

but when I bleed I do not cry or curdle

       cream or poison bread I am no bait to the bear

you cannot slay and yet you say I only breed

       blight upon your hallowed beds your holy tables

while still I stand atlas under all your fear and

       anger I am the sepulchre of your grins I take

all of you in I die for days that you may live

       I am the godhead you get but do not give

9

Said the River When I Begged for Her Song

I am the bending black silk
       debriding the knuckled spines

of winter I am the swollen
       kink brushing brown shoulders

of summer I am angel bone and braid
       kneading beaded areola

I am the long fall into a curve
       from ankle to ass I am that girl

woman mother and that old
       witch of ice I am tattoo of canal

my clavicle pierced by lock
       and bridge and flashpin I am

hot mud of lips I am wide roll
       of hips mossed kiss of clit

I poured flesh from this earth to wake
       you with wide-eye with whisper

with willow thighs and you come
       now to me all fist and ferry pole

all two-stroke motor drooling
       gas and oil you come again

with black powder and flywheel
        clock tower and loom

and build rooms of severed hymns
        milling silver out of cotton

limbed against any April melt. But I
        shall yet tumefy. I shall riot above

all bulwarks and towers and I shall drown
        your books and bearded lies.

Third Day, Friday, May 1, 1992

Dillon knew Shorty from juvie or wrestling
but I didn't know him at all not even from the halls
in between the bells but when Shorty snatched
Lori by her long red hair and started dragging
her around the parking lot his presence was
suddenly a fact and so too that he was black
and pissed over Rodney over cops over all
these white kids who thought they owned
this McDonalds' parking lot where his boys
rolled up with bats and clubs and stroked
real or feigned handguns in their hoodies and
circled around us that night as we sipped beers
and ate fries and why they rolled up in our spot
was all over the news as LA stayed detonated
for a third day but the point of maybe no return
was when Shorty took Lori who screamed
and kicked and his boys held up their sticks
if any of us started to move and we were scared
even the numbest of us knew this is how
it starts we'd seen enough of acting tough before
and what happens when there's no way out
except for through then pug muscled Dillon
jumped out Dillon whose folks were gone
who smashed a bottle over my neighbor's head
who missed part of the football season rocking
kiddy prison he jumped out and said Shorty Shorty
you don't want to do this man this is bad
I'm your friend you know me I'm your friend
this ain't the fucking way to end this man let
her go and we'll all take off and the parking lot

is yours and Shorty could have shivered Dillon
scalped Lori and could have taken all that mad
and burned the whole stage down but he didn't
no he let her go instead and Dillon hugged him
and helped Lori up and we white kids rolled out
rolled home where the fire for us was just on TV

Real Life

for E.W.

In *The Fighter* Wahlberg plays a welterweight
from Lowell named Micky Ward and Micky
one night, sticking up for his crackhead half-brother
Dicky, played by Christian Bale, gets his right hand
busted by the cops, just like in real life.

                      In the film
one of the cops is played by the real-life son of one
of the cops and he was, for his time, a cop in Lowell,
I played football with him in high school. I can still
see him all alone in the end zone after our tunnel-
visioned QB threw it to me again on a tight-end drag
for short-yard gain.

                 Great to see him play his dad,
though I heard there were issues between them,
and then to see him grin into the camera during
those closing credit shots of the town and people.
Hollywood had come to us to find a hero and though
I never met Micky I saw him once at the gym.

A few years later, well after the cameras tided out
of town, after Bale had made his Oscar speech,
Dicky got popped again for stealing and dealing
and the cop I played ball with drove home one night
so ripped he never saw the SUV as he veered across
Route 110 in Methuen.

A man named Bryant Paula
died instantly. The cop, the boy I knew, was arrested.
He wept in court, asked to be punished, and went to jail.

And none of this has anything to do with the movies,
except that maybe everything has to do with the movies
as we run alone into an October end zone, arms flailing,
hoping someone will see that we are more than our falling
action, more than this soft light flickering against the dark.

Saving Throw

after Robin Coste Lewis's "Math"

Take a boy. My boy. Understand mortality rates have been falling for decades. Understand there is no safer time to be alive. To be a boy. White boy. Blue-eyed son.

But understand there are three kinds of lies. Understand the anecdotal to be gospel.

Take a boy and assign a number to his flesh. Assume the number is his chance of being taken, world-murdered before he reaches manhood.

Assume that number is 18. Assume his dad has a twenty-sided die. To live, roll an 18 or higher. Assume the wicked of this exercise.

Now roll. Now adjust the roll for the variables:

Add for American not black, for American not brown. Add for not the city I grew up in and its downtown, its busses, its Olde E alleys behind liquor stores.

Subtract for his art. Subtract for his tender heart. Subtract for a velvet heavy velvet hot velvet breathless sadness. For sadness for why he feels so sad sometimes.

Divide for sex as gender, for who he is told he is by who he is supposed to love, who he might want to love. Divide him by love.

Subtract for our anger, our MAGA, our gaslit nostalgia, for what it might mean to be a man in a world frothing toward war.

Add for how rich. Subtract for how poor. Multiply by privilege, square by systemics. Fraction for fentanyl, COVID, for the PM 2.5 pushed into his lungs.

Add for no belt, no switch, no father's fist. Add for no pistol in the house. Subtract for lockdown drills, for AR-15s, bump stocks, Columbine copycats. Divide by the NRA, Big Pharma, bought lots at Yale and Harvard.

Take away for the hate you give, the villainy you teach.

Subtract for the anger of lost white boys. Subtract for the cruel white boys. Add for saintly boys in makeshift cathedrals.

Add for my thick back, my tears, my laugh. Subtract for my bark.

Add for Isaac. Subtract for Ishmael.

Add for the strength of women. For his mother's love that might be enough all on its own.

Take a boy. Take all the boys. Roll their bones.

Said the River When I Begged for His Song

So I may look so slicked back, bullet blue,
coolest dude under a root of summer swelt
that you want to step off yah stone and melt
yah meatstick face into all my cool,
my smooth wet place. But sometimes, kid (you seen
it!) I'm so jacked I don't need a hundred suns
turning to tongue bridges into cud.
Some days, so filled with all my rage and rain,
I rip this whole town down and wash it with stones,
blown tires, shopping carts, and boosted I-Rocs.
Then I burst over all those worn out locks
and sandbag banks to bumrush yah streets, yah bones.
I bully up the blocks, my whitewater wall
showing you just how ugly pretty I can call

out all the beat and broken ways you bit
my dirt with hammer and shovel, with reeking load
of angles and invention. And all for gold?
All to show yah more than that stack o' dimes dick,
that somehow you could run a train on death?
That's all kind of kiss my ass bullshit wrong.
And now you come sucking up for a song,
now yah kneeling and begging for my breath,
mumbling how yah so humbled in my mud,
making me some messed-up amalgam of mother
and lover, professing some mission to recover
the missing past and plasma of yah blood.
Screw you, kid. Should just put you over my knee.
That tough love you never got from yah daddy.

Tankas While Standing Near

the blue lipped river,
our pocket stones skipped,
we slurp first frappes of spring
as beater engine exhaust
carcinogens sidewalk weeds.

The Chevy's speakers
blast the Divinyls "I Touch
Myself" and Kelly
rolls her eyes, first at Randy,
then at me, we blushing boys.

So, Randy's into
Kelly and Kelly's into
me but I'm crushing
on nearly anybody
all depending on the week.

Kelly will become
a nurse, Randy a secret
service agent. I'm
a teacher, poet. It's so
wild that we become something

when March light's getting
low. Here, nights are still winter.
And we'll never love
each other like this again
after Randy drives us home.

On My Mom Showing Me that Photo of Gram and Aunt Althea in Blackface

What I want to say is that *our* sweet grandmothers
and *our* crazy great aunts went in blackface
to those minstrel shows, those weekend festivals,
fundraisers for Keith Academy in the 50s, and then got
their pictures mapped by light, because that's just
what was done then, all that anyone knew to do.
I want to say *our* grandmothers and *our* aunts
because I don't want to say *my* grandmother or
my crazy great aunt. I want my wrong being wrong
in armies of wrong, safe in hate's battalions, diluted
in the drench of blame, safe when I see photos
of them singing behind the dark, my mother
still a kid somewhere there laughing, not knowing
what bodies have been broken and sunk in rivers
from down the Tallahatchie to up the Merrimack.
Let me snuggle into a mob's dissolution of fault,
be history blown to dust and not this sin of salt.

Insidious

Because white men cannot police their imagination, black men are dying
                                             —Claudia Rankine

Sunday morning late May I love the maples
      this time of year over Andover Street
the bright green budding the sun seeming to hang
      its light on leaves that canopy
            across the busy pothole road
onto which I've turned my truck my children in the back
      as we head home north
            to New Hampshire leaving
my in-laws waving on the lawn I wonder if my kids
will see these trees like I see them
            without the days
on days growing up here but they are talking laughing
      as I hit the radio seek from Red Sox
          highlights to NPR and

Sunday morning late May I love the maples
      I doubt my kids notice as I do the teenage boy
         with long purple-patched hair pulled
back into a bun above his backpack
         but I do I see him
walking down the sidewalk I walked down so many
      times in my life and I wonder
         if he lives around here if
he does that's good it's good that the neighborhood
      be more mosaic and it's important that a boy
         a black boy
can walk down my old street and not meet with people
      hassling him for his color or his clothes and oh

Sunday morning late May I love the maples
            how I know there are those
watching him from behind their shutters and blinds
        staring out through double paned windows
            seeing this boy and seeing only his blackness
wondering whether he belongs here and certainly some
            think he doesn't and someone may even call the cops
        their fear oxidized into anger and so this kid
                maybe just headed down to the White Hen
            to hit the deli and a grab a Coke could get hassled
                and all for what
        for being black for his clothes because he's big
almost chunky and the moms around here love their skinny
        kids and skinny diets and my god

Sunday morning late May I love the maples
        the nerve of their notions
of what is normal what is comfortable is deplorable but
        what if someone does call the cops
it would be so awful for suddenly blue lights
        twirling a siren belch a short blast
            so this poor kid would be asked and harassed
        but I would certainly pull over
definitely defend him and say *Leave this boy alone!*
            although I mean it's possible his backpack's full of weed
                for the neighborhood kids but this
            is terrible of course for me
to even think and if I saw a cruiser roll up on him I would
        pull over and say something I'm sure I would yes

Sunday morning late May I love the maples
        I'm sure I'd be brave if it was safe
with my children sitting in the back but I truly would try
       to at least slow down and say something like
        All you see is his blackness and this is all
you see! because of course I see more I really do and I know
        how hard it must be to be him I'm sure I do because
     I'm one of the good ones I am right I really am
and then the boy fades from my rearview mirror his head
     rising from the sidewalk slab to see my maples

     or are those elms I wonder
my whole life I've been so sure they were maples

   but maybe they're elms maybe they

        have always been elms

The Adorned Fathomless Dark Creation

for Joe Meehan

That a woman calculated light could be drawn
                     from collected radio frequencies

so that this world could see the shadow, the sink,
                     the portal out of our observable universe,

that this was all over the headlines the day
                     we would wake the man that had been

husband, father, grandfather to two children,
                     that tiny bees were found in some other woman's eye,

feeding off her tears after she'd been plucking
                     weeds from graves during Qingming,

that, before today, black holes existed only as gaps
                     in data, as engines that turned existence

around their absence, that before today his absence
                     was never a presence and none of us knew

about the sweat bees that nest near graves, inside
                     fallen trees, subsisting on pollen and nectar

but also, on our salt, so that as our children kneel
                     beside his casket, maybe it's not the loss,

not the gut empty sick that only death can gift,
                not the singularity that swallows all,

everything, even light, maybe there's no weeping,
                maybe it's only some bees blurring their sight.

Legend

Recall the frayed red corduroy robe
and him, my grandfather,
in wide armed wooden chair, in Lowell,
the kitchen where my mother

grew up, the Highlands, Wilder Street,
around us. Now he's laughing,
watching me dance for him, a foot
shod in black leather tapping

out a memory or just some story
given to me by my mother.
My uncle said Gramp called me Csonka
because my thick toddler

thighs were like that Dolphins back.
And Gramp was sick by then
so all I knew of him was a robe
below a nose broken

seven times between high school
and Green Bay. On my wall,
a photo of him in his Packers gear
sitting with Curley Lambeau,

(posing as if to recapture
something that was candid
a second ago) before the war,
two daughters, before he quit

the NFL to coach, to become Coach,
before state champs, coaching
his son, before working Sundays
at the florist, before telling

my father *No*, before the cancer
and the July day at a rented
house in Seabrook when he said,
Take care of my wife, to my dad

just days before he died. And this
was a life, spun out from frames
of photos and fuzzy anecdotes,
like him playing semipro games

under a pseudonym to send
money home during the Depression
while on a full ride at Fordham,
or sitting on the can

in Lambeau's locker room he heard
his coach come in and say
We need to sign this Riddick kid
and held out till they paid

him five hundred more a year.
Or that meet in high school
when he figured the angle of descent
from the hole in the wall

how far he'd thrown the shot.
And all of this gets spun
though jennies of local history
myths carried out by sons,

carried into legends looming
around us, measuring us
against our most impossible ghosts.
I can't even recall his voice.

Uncle Ray, who must have sounded
like him, is gone now too,
and the way the men in my family
die young in beige cold rooms

of antiseptic light warps
like whispers woven through
a sick-lipped joke. And these deaths
dissolve our boyhood, weigh

us down as men, as much of that
as we can bend to and still
not break. So as men we learn
to doubt the folklore trill

of our fathers' lives, that no spotlight
fixed on them as either hero
or villain, that neither they nor we
stand protagonist in this play.

For there were mothers and aunts,
cousins, too, drifting through,
all slipping offstage to die in a letter
becoming, *Oh, no, did you*

hear who just passed? at some Sunday brunch
with your disinterested kids.
On the wall of the high school fieldhouse
his name, Raymond E. Riddick,

remains. I recall the dedication,
that building as new and Gram
alive, my mom so proud, the town
honoring their sinewy legend

and I was only seven then.
But I recall ten years
later Chris Lyman laughing, *Must suck
to have that kind of pressure,*

the fuckin' gym named after him,
like you even had a choice
about being any good?
growled in his wise-ass voice.

I don't know how I felt that weight
but loved that he, the best
athlete in school, empathized,
saw me, even if just

more headlines to be whittled away
by sports page stats that can't,
that don't, ever know the story
between trick play and punt.

And where slipped Coach from all of this?
Ephemeral in my life
as in these lines, the man loses
out to the myth each time

I try to conjure something truer than
some story of him with Jack
Kerouac or pissing next
to John Wayne, the Duke,

truer than the hurt of his daughters
still missing their dad, truer
than the stiff-hipped old men who stop
me (yet, less each year)

to say they loved him, how he made
them men. So, whatever
else he may have been, this
seems where it wants to end, where

rough-hewn nuances of life fade.
I guess it's best to just
print the legend. They'll build a new
high school, that field house

bulldozed along with his name. We who
are left will forget and thus
we are what is forgot, highlight reels
lost to dust. All of us.

Conditional

If skin is the first lie
our bones will learn to tell

then we are bags of broken
looms. If architects

of tongue left a dream
of language on your eyes

then only the pricked
fingers will decipher our rot

of rose. If morning
won't let go the cuticle moon

your slippers will hush us away
in a bloom of snow

that creases the black mud
of our canals. When copperheads

ask to milk the stone what's
gone cold is what we've never known

of old park benches and rusted
out Fords. Here the fur

of lists sheds on the front yard couch.
Here, finger this spark, the first

gasp of galaxy. In here I'm the last
best flesh I'll ever hold.

Said the River When I Begged for Their Song

and whatever the man called each living creature,
that was its name

—Genesis 2:19

Very well,   call me   river

    Call me Merrimack   track me back   to Pemigewasset   to
      Winnipesauke.

      Call me   mother   father   and apron strung

deep lunged

              lover.   Call me   confluence,

      call me flood and   slug   name me strong place and

          bathe me into fable.

Dance me out as your tradition   your tributary.

      Construct me as your creation myth.

           Sing my hair of braided salmon,

map my curves,   my cock, my cunt,   my noting, my not.

      Mark this salinity,

  paint my Pawtucket Falls   and survey

      my alluvial belts of stone.

    Drag my gut for your stolen cars,   your suicides,   your sediment.

Define me by your dams and your damned.   Denotate my silt   detonate

    my banks   so I bleed and braid you with canals.

Swim out, son of man,   with brush of lips.

You'll never find me in your box of words,   your book of failed verbs,

for I too wide,   I too winding,   I too glass of sky,

and you will drown for this kiss

on your swallowed tongue   and idiom.

II

There is no way to get lost
If you simply follow the river

—from *The Popol Vuh*
translated by MICHAEL BAZZETT

River Valley Hexaëmera

after Brandon Courtney

LUNAE

What happened was Laurentide ice ripped back like lightning
        dragged its ass north tearing loam from stone

stitching lenticular hills of till birthing drumlin
        after drumlin calving kettle ponds and vining

eskers across the earth like 'roid-roped veins
        and then came water shaking off the shaggy freeze

bursting for the sea again and the river our river rolling down
        from white mountains got bent against granite

and turned a hard tangle toward the east to reach
        the rip and tide and up and down its banks were birch

and ash and wolf and bee cuz sunlight lit upon the gulping
        dirt at last all funk and fecund and by first evening

first tribes moved their breath upon the shore
        called the water Merroh Awke sang it Strong Place.

MARTIS

Called the water Merroh Awke sang it strong place
        and in the spring when herring and sturgeon returned

when salmon walked up waterfalls they Pennacook they Wamesit
        they Narrangansett Amoskeag and Pawtucket

left grudge and axe in the grass and dove for the catch
        they drank in bamegizegak they talked of saba

they tracked spring deer from dawn through late summer
        harvested the fall for winter and spoke of pale men hailing

down with their sideways sick and firesticks and sagamore
        Passaconaway saw when their boats first landed and now old

he tells his people they must bend against the storm that the wind
        blows hard that the old oak shakes and its branches

are gone and its sap is frozen it bends it falls he says
        peace with the white man is his final command.

MERCURII

Peace with the white man is His final command cuz God
      is a motherfucker hell we hammered canoes into coffins

just by coughing in the river so by the time we carried our bibles
      up their banks whole villages were empty but for some bones

with soil already sewn and pools of jumping shad we only had
      to kick the still seething coals to get our fires going

while our kids played with dolls left behind by other days and days
      rolled on we figured ways to kill the Indian and still stay Puritan

damn King Phillip practically made us a country or rallied us rebellious
      enough to dunk a different king and then came a big ass canal

from the Merrimack down to the Charles and water was a will to power
      especially when Lowell used the five-fingered discount to build a textile

make us industrial then planned a town that taps that ole Pawtucket ass
      to power the loom that we let a woman work at every day.

Power the loom they let me work at every day save
        the Sabbath save my soul if I have to listen to that schika

taka shika tak machine shuttle through me from dawn to dinner
        but debts are due on father's farm and really there is great fun

with these women although the rooms are small and six to a bed
        but oh to talk and rest my head on her warm hip when the whip

of winter snaps the river when the hours go on forever
        as we barter our flesh and hours for a dollar consumption

is a factor last week a child lost a finger and yesterday our pay
        was cut and now these papists these French and Irish

even worse these unhorsed Greeks slip through the brick
        and take our labor but we really we must all stand together

against the way the work and wages worsen so from toxic dust
        upon our tongues chant we want bread and roses too.

Upon rough tongues the shout for bread and roses too
              spreads up and down the river from Lawrence to all

the valley so every weaver tubercular fevered and hung
              with hunger stood in bullets bare toed to the winter even

as mill boss cops beat down mothers until at last the strikers
              got what we wanted if only for a while cuz then the IWW

moved on to hotter headlines and the bosses whittled us away
              and then the war and even more of them took jobs south

and suddenly this town was down like too many others
              looked like the Kaiser bombed us to brick and cobble

so before The Bust we were already busted even another German
              phalanx of fuckery was only faintly felt by the 50s we were riding

gridiron gods Riddick and Plomaritis even some back named Kerouac
              just to have something to cheer for in damp November.

SATURNI

Just to have something to cheer for in the damp November
          of a city ain't no small thing and when new jobs come we make

a run of making it work but Wang flared out and gangs
          rolled in like the TRG and Latin Kings and new tribes fishing

for the American scene Brazilian Puerto Rican and Cambodian
          but still too many got lost on no jobs or dope but there was crack

you couldn't smoke a light in which the city woke to what it was
          what a valley could be where art and history

might be milled into handmaidens of hope and so
          a celebration of self sort of slipped in along with that flood

of oxycontin but that something sure ain't nothing and the river's
          cleaner than it's been for years the hawk and heron

are returning and even Hollywood showed up for Micky
          for real could a town and river ever be more like Ward v. Gatti?

SOLIS

Could a town and river ever be more Ward v. Gatti
      they way they pounded the way they danced they hugged

us into Sunday rope-a-dope rest to look upon the mess we made
      along our way to love or money and too many bodies rolled over

those falls and too much of earth that cannot be called back
      but maybe there's time here for breath and prayer

to name what's holy there and there before the burn of us
      is snuffed and perhaps there's no foot upon the treadle

no fingers at the loom just the random warp and weft before
      a doom unto which we will not know we moved

and all the beauty of seeing beauty will be tombed
      all sorrow for sins gone as dark as a sunless moon

but I am nightshade and I love the luster that comes last
      and the lightning way the ice rips back.

III

Lethe, the river of oblivion, rolls his watery labyrinth,
which whoso drinks forgets both joy and grief.

—John Milton, *Paradise Lost*

Winter Break

The season we unscrewed the trucks from decks,
rubbed crayon on their bottoms as wax and nailed
the scavenged loops of purple nylon belts
into plywood for bindings, chopping skateboards
into snowboards to bomb the golf course hills
the next town over.

                          The day my brother and I
waited out back of our house with Dave and Justin
for mom to drive us all too lazy to walk.

The second that I saw my brother's board
between his feet as I tightened my boots.

                                The hours
of my mother, sick of us at home all break
and listening to us grouse, *There's nothing for us
to do we're bored.*

                    That moment it took for me
to grab the board set on its side between
my brother's feet as I rose from laces to ram
it hard into his groin.

                        The forever for him
to fall howling into the snow as I
realized I'd hurt him more than the laughing mad
I'd hope to have.

How quick as shit Jon was
back on his feet, the board in his fist so fast
I never saw it smash the skull above
my smile.

The minute maybe until my head
stopped spinning, cheek boneraw bloody, until
mom detonated from the kitchen, her keys
a nest of prison shivs.

The hot half-life
of tears before she's yelling, *Get in the car*!

The time inside the time that silent ride
to Trull Brook's hills. Dave and Justin in tricky
terror of witness, Jon his aching crotch,
my eye a scabbing fire.

The years of failure
mom must have felt in her *Get out! Walk home!*

The four or five barreling runs we made
on junk-ass boards above that valley where
the river cracked the air with ice before

my brother and I were talking, then laughing, about
his balls, mom's sudden anger, Dave and Justin,

about why it was we had to break my face.

Ceremony Drowned

First-period bell screeched   like some wreck in the rain

     as I left home room lugging

        my maroon mesh bag

and saw two boys running

     with nunchaku and chain.

   Past folds of flesh and kindling sex,

        they cut a vein

through us all off to class

     to catch the kid they'd tag

midstride,   right in the skull,

     like a wreck in the rain.

       The boy being chased clawed past us,

       owl-eyed with pain

and then the whacks to his back and gut,

       the sudden gag.

   I'd never seen a beatdown

       by nunchaku and chain.

All three of the boys were quick, strong,

       Cambodian.

       It was a gang thing,

    about colors in a rag.

Sacred shitless to end like some wreck

                         in the rain,

I watched,   shuffled on.

              And by the time the cops came

      those two boys were gone,

                  maybe off having a drag

down by the canal.

             But that nunchaku, that chain,

   just keeps pounding meat

                    like a rusted-out refrain,

like the thread of a song

        that keeps catching a snag—

      that I watched a boy hurt

             by nunchaku and chain

and all I that didn't do

        won't reckon the rain.

Hannah in Effigy

Though she's all but forgotten today, Hannah Duston was probably the first American woman to be memorialized in a public monument. . . . The mystery of why Americans came to see patriotic "heroism" in Duston's extreme—even gruesome—violence, and why she became popular more than 100 years after her death, helps explain how the United States sees itself in world conflicts today. . . . The idea of a feminized, always-innocent America has become the principle by which the United States has structured many interactions with enemy others.
—Smithosian.com

But when I woke in stone my child
was nowhere nearer,

and Merrimack had dragged me back
to this atoll, this Boscawen.

My right hand holds the hatchet I used,
in my left the bouquet of flesh

I had taken from their heathen heads.
It is said my captors taught me how.

Is it easier for you that they murdered her,
my Martha, broke her baby skull

against an apple tree, plucked my nipple
from her root? The truth? I recall bare feet

on ice but not the apple tree. I was distraught,
though, at least enough for slaughter.

And does the ledger still stand in my favor?
How do the scalps tally? How many

were too many, how many until God
becomes our enemy? I was mother,

marbled down with milk in my breast.
That child was in me, my blood

still staunched by a napkin the night
my captors slept too deep.

I offer no apology, no justification
for their six children.

I was mother. I am mother, but no
matriarch to your concord of murder.

If you need to believe, if you need
my maternity, my femininity,

my goddess of liberty in your myth
of destiny, mouth of country,

will you forever let her head explode,
feel virtue in the long hair slipping wet

through my fingers? Will you question
why I collected on the bounty.

Misprision

after a poem by Richie Hoffman

After the erudite young have left me
alone with wine bottles emptied and poetry,

I look up the story of Hadrian's lover
for context into their conversation

and read that this Antinous is *defiled*
after death then worshipped as a god

and think don't we defile our gods
before they are dead, before we know

they are gods, need them as gods,
invent them into gods? Don't we eat

of the flesh and then condemn them
to death? But that's not right.

It's not *defiled*. It's *deified*. I misread
the small print. My eyes are going,

drifting into the deep right field
of middle age. I still see the waves

bump up on the horizon but misjudge
their movement to the shore.

And the menus seem darker than before.
I could get reading glasses, cheaters.

I could find a young lover like Hadrian
did and graft my belly to her smooth

skinned youth. She could read to me
and show me the pulsing of the waves.

I could get old and sick on top of her,
slump into her breasts and cast her

to the river of my rebirth. Then I could
write poems to her, name cities after her,

wall myself off from the barbarian cold.
I could sculpt her body from stone, from film,

from water. I could paint her in my image,
sated by all I had done to deify her.

A Brief History of American Labor

We did not call ourselves ladies. We did not forget that we were working-girls, wearing coarse aprons suitable to our work, and that there was some danger of our becoming drudges.

—Lucy Larcom, *A New England Girlhood*, 1889

So how they do is first they give her more
to do by rolling out two more machines
but slowing down each loom to 100 beats
a minute to mitigate the impact of working
two looms at once and this is what they called
back then *the stretch out* and once they stretch her out
once she gets good at working four at once
then comes of course *the speed up* to over
120 beats a minute and look
how good she's gotten making almost two
bucks more a month up from 14.50 hell
that's a 16% raise for increasing
output 70% and now the boss
can cut back labor and still linger along
the river summer evenings with his wife
and watch blue herons dollar-sign their necks
then fall into flight above the humming bricks.

Textile Triolet

schika tak schika taka schika tak schika taka schika tak schika taka schika tak **By these looms we lung the fiber of our hour** schika taka schika tak schika taka schika tak schika taka schika tak schika **spinning textiles into filament cirrus** schika tak schika taka schika tak schika taka schika tak schika taka schika tak schika taka schika **that flit between each ringing of the tower** schika taka schika tak schika taka schika tak schika taka schika tak schika taka taka schika schika tak schika **By these looms we lung the fiber** tak schika taka schika **of our hour** tak schika taka schika tak schika taka schika tak schika taka schika tak tak schika taka schika **upon this earth** schika taka schika tak schika tak schika taka schika tak schika taka schika tak schika taka **inside this machine** schika taka schika **roar!** tak schika taka schika tak **of groaning joints** schika taka schika tak schika taka schika tak schika taka schika tak schika taka schika tak schika tak schika taka schika tak schika taka **where no one can** schika tak schika taka schika tak schika taka schika schika tak schika taka schika tak schika taka schika tak schika taka schika tak schika **HEAR US !** taka schika tak schika tak tak schika taka schika tak schika taka schika tak schika taka schika tak schika taka schika tak schika taka schika tak schika tak schika taka schika tak schika **By these looms** tak schika taka schika tak schika taka schika tak schika schika tak schika taka schika taka schika taka schika tak schika taka schika tak schika taka **we lung the fiber** taka schika tak schika taka schika tak schika taka schika tak schika taka schika tak schika taka schika tak schika taka schika tak schika taka schika tak schika taka schika tak schika schika tak schika taka schika tak schika taka **of our hours** tak schika taka schika tak schika schika tak schika taka schika tak schika taka tak schika taka **our throats cottoned** taka schika tak schika taka schika tak schika tak schika taka schika tak schika taka schika tak schika taka schika tak schika taka schika tak schika taka **in one silent** schika tak schika taka schika tak schika tak schika taka schika schika tak schika taka **chorus** tak schika taka schika tak schika taka schika

To My Daughter at Thirteen

after Lynn Melnick's "Twelve"

When I was your age, I loved a girl named Jenn and when she had Becky ask me to come over that blue October afternoon to the house where she was babysitting and I slammed hard to the street bombing down a hill on my Jeff Phillips, one Kryptonic wheel catching a stone, my elbow all road rash and blood and when later I sat next to Jenn on the couch I think she expected me to kiss her but I wasn't sure and didn't know how to be sure so I played *Don't Break the Ice* with the kid she was sitting for. And wasn't I such a gentleman, a good boy, and so terrified of a girl? Delaney, your dolls, your Leias, your Reys look dusty on your bedroom shelf. When I was your age my GI Joes still posed but I was scared to play with them in case dad came home muttering *he's weird* to mom so when I was your age I made myself go outside to play football with my brother's friends. When I was your age I stopped talking to Reggie about the X-Men on the bus even though the fall of the mutants was upon us. When I was your age I finally figured out how to punch a boy back hard enough he wouldn't ever hit me again before school, on the blacktop, as I leaned against the chain linked fence that covered our backs from the knuckles and grabs of older boys. You tell me the cool girls are mean. You say you don't bother with them but have you been in love, brought to balefire in another's glance? When I was your age the girl I loved dumped me the night a ball went through Buckner's legs and the Sox would lose the Series and she kissed Dave. Is a broken heart still a hurt all over the skin? Is this what you and Mom are whispering? You've told me kids you know are kissing. When I was your age some friends were getting laid but I just wanted to be seven again and forever in Ms. Kew's class drawing pictures of Luke and Artoo. When I was your age we started sneaking beers because we were supposed to start sneaking beers but Delaney be safe, keep sitting on the den couch with us to argue and angle about what show we should all watch on a Friday night because when I was your age Friday night was football games, showing off to the girls by getting bloody in games of *Smear the Queer*, because when I was your age gay was AIDS and we were all too afraid to say anything but what we thought was the right thing. Oh, poor Reggie on the bus. When I was your age the only good thing I ever did was stick up for him that one time and Voula heard me and told him and he said thank you. But mostly when I was thirteen I was a coward like the rest while you statue outside your school to protest gun violence, while you draw pictures where every woman is the right kind of beautiful, while you get yourself up in the blueblack dawn for a world you know will come at you with claws, while you laugh with your brother, talk to your mother, while you lean into me and let me give you the hug I didn't even know I needed.

Sapphic

Merrimack snaking through sighs of craggy
floe and log, whispering that spring may shake blue
hair from out the hillocks' slow skull of winter.
Yet of the clawing

freeze and water streaming by banks and grasping
trash and rusted truck parts that sink though mud and
poison blood and bone, the black river flows like
nothing will matter,

happen, change, or even has ever been or
ever not been. Time may exist or it's some
cracked Edenic covenant, human built, and
just a machine that's

building machines, making all estuaries—
where our salted flesh seeks salinity, some
delta of eternity—lost,
trackless as divinity.

Zenith of a Given Place

Winter becomes a habit. And so does age.
Or aging, you could say. So slipping on
a coat, a hat, your gloves—it's just routine.
And staying warm is standing still in beige
thermal socks, waiting for your bus to groan
through Thursday's slush to push you back to work—
some shitty desk with a view of a manmade lake
you watch freeze over from your padded foam
chair in some office park outside Tewksbury.
Who wouldn't want the warmth of Buffalo wings
washed back with Buds while a Hooters girl sings
Happy Birthday again? Eternity
might be knowing some dust has died and some
stars have not while waiting for the check to come.

Getting Out

So seeing morning   so the drunks   the morning

so seeing drunks lined up   seeing morning lined up

along a rainbow so seeing drunks lined up at the Rainbow

Lounge seeing the theater   the triple X's   so seeing

XXX   so seeing those men in ragged coats

so ragged coats   so ragged men   ragged faces

like laughing leather   so seeing September   seeing her son 16

so seeing the river   driving over the river   so the river

rushing over truck tires   her tires rumbling the bridge

so her son 16   the boarded-up mills   the half skulled

factories   so her son 16 she wept   so she left him

to this town   so this is college   this so far away

from their two-family house   Pittsfield gone   so the river

so she wept   so that is all we heard of her   so my father

told us his goals after college   to turn thirty   so serious

so business   and to get out of this town   so easy   so much time

left   so way past thirty when he showed us the scrub

near the water   near the truss bridge dieseled above

where he puked his first screwdriver   so his last   so what

we didn't know what a screwdriver was   so much yet

in what we didn't yet   so many rides homes from soccer

games   so many Saturdays   his stories on the road that rivers   road that rivers by the river   so the river

near a closed theater   near a lounge   near a college   so near

the hospital   so we sat by him that Sunday   so gone the Sundays

laying next to him watching westerns   so a house also gone

so work trips to Seoul   so Tokyo   so Dallas and Pennsburg

a million frequent flyer miles   so 63   so much time   so sick

the hospital   the hospital he watched us being born   where we

watched him die   so close the pop and groan   so close

the groan   the breath of ice floes   gun grey the slush

along the road   so the river   so the road   so close the water

the close water   his mother   so the water

so the water his mother wept to let him go   so let him go

Oh Father, Your Fear

Draped to his waist in other milk he came
to civilize and not to conquer he is forever

covenant with best intentions and swore
on Friday he would not get angry but Sunday

was a long car ride home with all the tears
tissued down into weeping silence how to keep

it as beautiful is what keeps it from being
beautiful he thinks crowds will gather to see mist

in the valley but to wade into it is as anonymous
as an echo dragging a yellow flower through

the river is it that he is too tired or too afraid
to blink into the oil of his own machine

so instead he smears fingerprints in liquid crystal
across aluminosilicate and wonders is this the last

we he will have here in this dirty cab of a pick up
horrified by Monday looming noticing how big his boy's

hands have gotten how she'll look her hurt straight
into his eyes and never not once ever blink.

Age of Discovery

Colonialism hardly ever exploits the whole of a country.

—Frantz Fanon

We did nothing to make those kids hate us, the four or five Puerto Rican boys who strutted up to the busted fountains by Kennedy Plaza where we were skating between section eight housing and city hall you know, just skating— my buddies, brothers, and I—grinding concrete corners of marble benches, redbrick steps, railings of wheelchair ramps—all we lacked up our hill of just cut grass and dad-helped half-pipes slid so snug between hemlock and blacktop. We did nothing to make them hate us, those boys, who walked over, rough dressed, wild haired, hard brown shoulders muscling through Lakers and Knicks tanks. My crew closed ranks, at first, just in case, but we did nothing to make them hate us. Soon all of us were hanging out, talking easily with these boys who didn't go to our school, who didn't have Bones Brigade decks, Gullwing trucks, Vision shorts, Vans kicks, and Slimeball wheels so good for carving across paved roads and emptied autumn pools. We said nothing to make them hate us. One boy, the biggest, rode a rusty beater bike and he jumped the same steps we ollied over. We laughed, trying to outtrick each other. And everyone was chill and the sun stayed out past eight and the breezes of coming summer swirled. I missed what set it off, who said or did the thing to make one of them, their youngest, hate us. But suddenly he suckered our youngest, my brother Paul, in the nose. By the time I looked up from a failed kick flip Paul was bleeding, holding his face, so I skated up to the kid and snatched his Yankees cap and dumped it in a puddle. To get even, not to start a fight, not to make them hate us. Their biggest sprung from his bike and got chin to chin with me, his hot breath yelling about his cousin's cap. He wanted me to swing, to bring it, sling it, but I didn't, wouldn't, couldn't. He punched my puffed-out chest, my ratatat heart learning to lean forward into his fist. What the fuck we do to make them hate us? I locked my jaw, tried to look mad, knowing that if I threw a punch all this would end bad. We would lose and I would lose, and I would have to beg him to stop in front of my friends and brothers who thought I was the tough I was pretending to be by giving this kid the satisfaction of a scrap, letting him shove me, even though he couldn't quite push me back. But he never threw a real punch either. Why not, I could never figure. Then an even bigger kid came from around a corner—their littlest kid had gone to get him. And this kid looked a man, thick muscled, bearded from neck to nose and rising against the dusk. We did nothing to make them hate us. Their man advanced. And that's when we knew to dance, bail and bolt into the stale of city hall. We found the room where the school committee met in all their suits and skirts, in all their faces pale as powder, where parents from the up the hill were trying to kill a bill ending all our rec sports. We ran to my mother and tried not to be noticed. Quivering at her feet we watched for those boys to muscle in, to drag us back into their downtown. But they never did find us. They likely never tried. Mom asked what made us run inside. She scowled at us, asked what we must have done to make them hate us.

Then I Let the Alpine Play

Just 15, all he could think was *No* when the cop
snatched his fake ID and started cuffing him so Paul
turned and tossed that down-lo five-O into a stand
of Bud Light cans and then tore ass like a bullet
out of the state border Pelham liquor store and past
his pals cranking Cube in Danny's granddaddy's white
Olds waiting on their 40s, just a crew of white
boys in snow hats acting all gangsta. By then the cop
was up and after him but the kid had booked it past
the parking lot and into the mosquito trees. Paul
climbed a barb fringed fence never thinking a bullet
might burn through branches but knowing he didn't stand
a chance if that cop caught up so he headed for a stand
of pines where he saw some house lights shine white
in the distance. By now his pals were shitting bullets
trying to rip out of the parking lot. Doubling back, the cop
pounced on their hood. Those bad boys gave up Paul's
name and number Hershey-squirt quick. No getting past
that cop. No kid had ever tossed him so dude was past
being pissed. Trying to get some girls to understand
why they should let him in the house to use the phone Paul
was sweating out whatever charm he had left in his white
toothed grin and fear flushed face. About then the cop
called this punk's house. I answered. He barked bullets
and didn't believe I wasn't my brother. "Bull! Let
me talk to your old man!" he spat and passed
on what happened and then this gravel-glottis cop
starts going off on how Paul was going to stand
trial for assault, resisting, flight. I wondered how we'd white
wash this to Mom cuz I bought the fake ID for Paul

in the first place. Then he hung up. That's when Paul
called me from a Dunks (hardly a place where bullets
and badges wouldn't gather). He was E.T.-in-the-river-white
when I picked his ass up. We doctored a story to get past
my role in all this. Little bro couldn't stand
me getting pinched too. Next day, after she called the cop,
Mom, appalled, took him in to bite that ole bullet.
He copped a plea, got probation. No having to stand
trial, risk juvie. Free pass. All so black and white.

Ars Poetica

How to recall that industrial maroon carpet home
room overpacked public high school stink of shit
weed dip spit blood pencil shavings armpit
How to bring back the boy who sat in the back
corner every morning quiet Cambodian kid
How to remember his face his voice his name
years later or even days later oh what we didn't see
How to talk about how he was shot walking home
and at school the next day made it our drama
How to be shot walking home from chess club
to find out we even had a chess club that met after last
bell when I'd drive an old Buick out to practice
How to be caught up in a whiskey pom-pom narrative
of football games, parking lot brawls, which packy
wasn't checking IDs or being watched by the cops
How to imagine him walking home across the lot
where the Gervais family once had that car dealership
How to imagine that lot where my dad bought a Buick
not the one I drove but that long white station wagon
How to be that all alone boy as a car rolled up
I picture that Olds full of kids who crowbarred Jamie
How to kill a friend trying to quit a crew the Tiny Rascals?
Asian Boyz? I think about that time some buddies of mine
came at me at a city pool for thinking I'd ratted them out
How to be a kid and quit that life and have to bleed for it
and hearing from a history teacher he was a smart kid
and wanted to go to college and get out of here
How to bleed out alone into that potholed cement
I almost cracked an axle cutting through there once
How to be cooked into a cautionary tale for white kids

See what happens? and their moms *Can't they just fit in?*
How to be a mother at home weeping for a son
carried it turns out from one killing field to another
How to be called *gook* and feel small and afraid
because we pick on a *him* but steer clear of *them*
when letter jackets harass you just like their daddy cops do
How to be next morning whispering *He sat over there*
and look how we circle up to sigh and hug each other
How to forget his name how to never really know
and never really try to find out beyond Googling gang
slayings that happened in Lowell in '92 for a damn poem
How to do a half-ass autopsy on his brief headline of history
and rivet his corpse onto the backfat of my memory
How to peddle in flesh and colonize his death

Where One Starts From

roots in the river's bluegreen pitch
of a heat bug's back

in redbrick mills rubied placental
sundressed in cirrus

and canals brown in willow shade
creaming in the patches

of light winging between leaves
and the concrete stories of Greek

revival Victorian revival Renaissance
revival and the busses that nuzzle

into bus stops and skaters shkblunk
sidewalks and a bottle that falls

from a buggy and the fingers that brush
it off and the coffee shops

shouting for names rushing past
and already the oregano dough

behind pizzeria glass and eggs
slip spitting on grills

and pork frying from the Thai joint
bread groggy from a bakery

and click of heels and thump of boot
sneaker squeak and scrape

of flops all the offices of Monday
of late May of what may be

of sometimes any morning might
surprise with possibility

as the crosswalk clock ticks off
how much of this light is left

When I Am My Brother Fishing with Deron

Shirtless, so our chests and shoulders,
     thick roped

        from throwing and lifting,
would tan in the sun, we—
          too young
to know we would never be this beautiful
again—

     split a thirty of Millers, a tin of Kodiak,
on the wobbly upper deck

         of a rented beach
house in the hot fat wind of July and tie

a red kite, the cheap and plastic dollar
store type, to the line

        of a spinning reel
and let it out. And out. Let it climb

offshore gusts above fanbox cottages,
     over dune grass, sand, all littoral limits,

        let it swim
up the sea of sky beyond cirrus and sight.

      And now I string lines
to wonder why.   To feel the long pull

when we reeled it back in,
to taste where it had been?

                    To wrestle
the muscle of wind? Or were we

                         drifting bait
for something more, angling angels,

          back trolling Gabriels as the deck
motored beneath the low okta

                    of clouds? Maybe
we clung to a beer hazy hope

                    to hook some
larger leviathan, something big enough

                    to bite
and fight and finally break free,

so that later on we could brag
                    all about the god that got away.

Arthur's

What's painted on the side says Paradise,
but this is Arthur's Diner no matter whose
spatula cracks eggs into the hissing spit

of ham and bacon frying on the grill,
in that little kitchen with just enough headroom
behind the counter to go mad. But Arthur,

he sang, all morning long, making Boott Mill
Sandwiches while Dot, his wife, miserably took
your order as if she hoped it was the last,

her eyes so sad for all her days inside
an idle train car where construction crews
and kids cutting class from the high school

sat on stools, shoulder a shoulder, breathing grease
on Herald headlines about the Sox, Celts and Pats.
Now Arthur's gone, dead not long after Dot.

And Artie Jr. sold the place then left,
I think, for Florida. But it's not so easy
erasing place and so the new face flipping

burgers becomes the booths and Formica, the cheese
stacked in diamond towers for peeling's ease,
becomes the guy pretending not to see

the students cockroach to the basement when
the cops raid the restaurant for truants
who can't afford to bust parole again.

Slathering butter on French toast, he exists
as someone else's Arthur or Al or Ed.
And the diner insists itself beside the river

always younger than the water, but
more ancient as well, heavy with the sink
of chipping paint, of taped up ducts dumping

their rainbowed grease into the Eastern Canal.
It sits shadowed in the hip of the mill,
as if it wished this street of winter potholes,

more propped shack than greasy spoon, painted
black, with window panes bloodshot when caught
inside the dawn. This place, for me, a stove

during those biting rains of March I worked
landscaping lawns, pretending the work was work
I was supposed to do, probably taking checks

from guys basically living in their shoes
so I could be blue collar for a season
or two. And I worked hard and I worked long,

busted my ass for whatever buddy was
my boss that spring through fall. But I could quit,
would not have to cut and haul and thatch until

at last there was nothing left of my back.
Twenty years later, Arthur's new owner slaps
a plate in front of me: the butter-grilled roll,

homefries, egg and triple meat of Arthur's
famous and delicious. *Who am I if it tastes
no good?* I think. *What am I if it does?*

Echo Tourism

Wind wracks the limbs, lightning
scars the birch and we burrow

in the scrub by the mill
where mud is still the riverbank

from the last time
we made it rain like this. There's rattle

in the leaves, in levers
left to settle in the mortar

and granite of tunnels, turbines,
in the rule of a tower bell.

Perhaps this is all
we've to come to expect

in all the cotton sugar can spin,
all the tubercular threads

risked in a shuttle's kiss, the way
we're thrown out only to warp

back in. Me, I kept wanting
my redbrick river of city, kept

climbing through it to finger
all its cantilever

and cobblestone, its locks
and its syringe lit bones.

But it just kept growing,
like grass mantling graveyards,

spooling out beyond my toes,
until it disappeared completely.

IV

The Merrimac River, broad and placid, flows down to it from the New Hampshire hills, broken at the falls to make frothy havoc on the rocks, foaming on over ancient stone towards a place where the river swings about in a wide and peaceful basin, moving on now around the flank of the town, on to places known as Lawrence and Haverhill, through a wooded valley, and on to the sea at Plum Island, where the river enters an infinity of waters and is gone.

—Jack Kerouac, *The Town and the City*

A Crack of Light

I

Roosting in a December dusk,
Fort Hill, Lowell, mimetic mill town

in the gloam, coveting some dark
plain, snow falling, gently as factory

ash, my back to Shedd Park's unlit swings
and slides, ballfields, and a cemetery

drawered in an incisored ice,
I catch, on a ripped lip of roadsalt wind,

a downtown that sirens, serrates
across the bony air. Through knuckled

trees and the arthritic angles
of triple-deckers, down Rogers Street,

over the valley of millbrick condos
and factory restaurants, of bridges

and churches, of section eight row houses,
I see, above a glaciated canal

the Christmas lit redbrick smokestack
masted above the Wannalancit Mills.

Tented by 5000 green bulbs hung hot
on cables from the blacklipped

chimney mouth, the smokestack glows
bright as any heathen holiday,

severe as some steampunk carnival,
against the sudden evening closing in

around vinyl siding and sagging pines,
all blurring into shadows, into profiles

where drag of cell tower and cable,
where crack of cobblestone and blacktop

soften in the dust dimmed starlight
of streetlamps and windows

all waking up now into a suppertime cue
of LCD blue.
               And in centrifuge,

the festooned smokestack of a textile mill
rechristened for Merrimack's last red

king to be exiled for god. The city flywheels
around the smokestack as on a glittering

spoke, spinning under moon creamed
clouds back into a dream of a past

we won't get past, this we a town, this town
a nation in miniature hanging its blades

over every block. Incandesced by Farley White
Company to be a communal Christmas tree

with twenty-foot star, the chimney, a searchlight
of Bethlehem, singes the skyline,

cold lights the river in stark reflection,
leading no wandering wise men to anything

but an old mill no longer a mill, a tree that is
not a tree, a sachem unmanned,

sealed so no flue-gasses blow or bellow
to rub yellow knuckles into the clock

tower back, all time cards now mud
for barbeled carp. Tonight it glows

in a kind of hallelujah green, electric
in its muddled cocktail,

its babel stalk of late industrial might,
junky affirmation, and watchtower

delight of half-asleep children praying
for a humbacked sleigh to fall from heaven.

II

But today is a day past the nativity
and now that electric tower gussets all of us

into the New Year, like the last lit candle
of Christmas night's sempiternal swindle,

corposant that lures me, my eyes
tugged on its hook, its list of histories

I can't make out in the watery dark
but which rewild me like a child whiskey-

eyed on the spitfire of a toy trolley.
In a breath, a blink, I could be downtown,

leaning under the chimney, over a canal,
cracks in the ice wide enough for me

to fall through and forever forget and be
forgot. And why not? The feeds we fat on

howl our time on this spine of ablated ice
is ticking down in lockdown drills, emptied vials

of Narcan, and the runoff legacy of textile dyes.
Then the ice will return, an adagio creeping,

and we will drumlin, turn glacial flour,
be once more unmolded moraine,

unparadised from all dust and breath,
beyond the scouring of this anthropic hour.

But digression doesn't diminish this—
the so still and so beautiful of the hill,

of this winter pitch of old growth elm and birch,
at the edge of the old millboss mansions,

in air so raw I could convince myself
I'm clean again, in rebirth again, my blood

busting oxygen, endorphins, meaning just
a Lucky rolled between index and thumb.

III

Tomorrow, my son will turn ten.
The boy of him is thinning from his chin.

His shoulders are widening, the earth
under him is his to hold and yet his eyes—

oracular on some sadness still to come.
What in all of this can I give him

but flat feet, football games, and the misspelt
names of long dead Indians?

What's his birthright but theft, desecration
of this dirt and every flesh? To my daughter

I may, or must, bequeath fallen empires
of cotton, gun powder gods, mass miracle

epidemics, the poisoned veins of engines,
ploughed-under marshes, dirty canals

of aborted labor, and the last plague
poured, finally, into the human river.

This the condition of mine and time.
By God's word we planed this palm of soil

down to its tendons. And now, nine parts weep.
And now grunts Cain's blue-eyed tribe

as we seek answers for the sins we sewed
in the shadows of slumbering volcanos.

IV

Dear God, was this your intent? Dear God
of wine and breath, I waited for you

in the pussy willows when my answers
got me kicked out of Sunday School.

But you didn't show. I played alone
in kiss of catkins throwing stones to broach

casks in the Concord's April ice. You are no more
than a strophe of flint on steel.

Your good news may have moved toward life
but we became a book of Dis and Leviticus.

And now to say I'm sorry for our history
becomes a too convenient apology

for those bricks stacked on brown backs,
and mortared by young girls' blood.

Look, here on this hill above Indian Ditch,
the Great Bear's son, Wannalancit,

last sachem of the Pennacook, broke
the Mohawk, preached his father's peace

when Metacomet scorched the colonial twilight.
And still his land was stolen and his bones

at last he hauled from his Wickasee Island,
where now Vesper Country Club looms.

Yet it is these bones that bring me
to my own, to all the others entombed

in these towns, this time. Now is the hour
for redress, to spin from the distaff

something more than the past's rough weave,
more than the allotted bolt of Lowell,

yet I'm pulled into my own, my filament.
It's all so much to rewind and try to untouch.

And so, to cut the belly and slip this mortal
helix has a certain eventide allure

as I trudge up this frost skulled hill
and climb the cemetery fence.

                             Carved from marble,

a perched white lion meditates upon a plinth
just beyond the wrought iron gate

of this necropolis. I imagine him quickened,
lit into life by this winter moon. Then maybe

he'll take me by the throat down this hill
to the Pawtucket Falls and fling me

like a rose into the ice floes of the Concord
where, like Thoreau, I will meet

the Merrimack. But then to float on, past
Lawrence and Haverhill, past the violence

of a season violently failing, finally rattling,
and slide north beyond Newbury and Deer Island

to be swallowed by upstreaming stripers,
daggered by beaks of returning blue

herons, a siege of them gutting me
under Key Bridge, beyond Gangway Rock,

shat out past Plum Island, my annihilation
tossed into the rim of the Atlantic at last

to become blur of sky and ocean,
become equal parts krill and leviathan.

But no. Again the river bends me back and now
the night's cold has its cost. Ossification

in ears and mucus stalagmite, corneas
of black ice collision. No, I can't stay lost,

tip out from this cradle yet, in this the minute
of my movement.

Already I'm not alone

in the dark. Lamplit windows silhouette
the shapes of bentbacked survivors,

shadows standing over stoves and tables,
struggling up the steep of stairs,

shadows in relief along the street holding
open doors, waiting for busses,

banking on any gospel of possible,
looking for a fix in the alley or the aisle,

saints as good as any others,
miracles of laughter, tears, and of try,

who sometimes even blessedly see each
other as they lean into flogging gusts,

booting over salted sidewalks to go home
or head out or just find reason

to move forward against the gullet
dark of scoliotic December.

V

So if now is a wound that will not heal
and all of our fingers slick upon the pommel,

red on a shuttle thrown between this weft,
this we woven through one warp of earth,

then all I can do is love you. All of you. And let you
love me. Allow for a faith in the lightning strike

of synapses, that there is some truth
laced through the bacterial rub of microbes.

Down the valley, the smokestack bulbs
glow suddenly warmer now,

each a crack of light in the long night,
one for every thousand garish, audacious,

useless, perfect life that receives
few prophets, less prophecy, and still insists

against the ghosts, though we know we'll fail,
will fall to frost, to fire, to fade.

Then the hacking of an IROC engine
crawling into the park as some kid slides

up to its window to buy a dime bag rips
me from winding through all this wool

to recall the touch, the taste, of kin
and kindred who will hold out a while longer

in their soft lit houses, in rusted trucks and rail
cars, in late-met classrooms and early-hour

barrooms, in church basement meetings
and in the tattered bedrolls under a weeping

willow, for me, for each other, to fumble
toward grace, toward all the light we have left.

ACKNOWLEDGMENTS

Many thanks to the following journals and venues that published these poems, some in different forms and under different titles.

Carolina Quarterly: "Invocation at the Merrimack" and "Zenith of a Given Place"

Narrative: "Ceremony Drowned" and "Oh Father, Your Fear"

Birmingham Poetry Review: "Said the River When I Begged for Her Song," "Eve, Bumming a Smoke on a Porch in Pawtucketville," "When I Am My Brother Jon Fishing with Deron," "Crack of Light," and "Ars Poetica"

Massachusetts Review: "A Brief History of American Labor"

Gulf Coast: "Where One Starts From" and "Conditional"

Green Mountains Review: "Then I Let the Alpine Play," "While Standing Near," and "Misprision"

Hippocampus Magazine: "Age of Discovery"

Tupelo Quarterly: "Third Day, Friday, May 1, 1992"

Nimrod International: "Arthur's," "Boys Beyond Spring," "Getting Out," "The Adorned Fathomless Dark Creation," and "Legend," published as winning poems in the Pablo Neruda Poetry Prize.

"River Valley Hexaëmera," published by the *Poetry by the Sea Conference,* was selected by Marilyn Nelson as winner of their sonnet crown contest.

Prime Number Magazine: "Insidious"

The Common: "Autobiography"

Split Rock Review: "Echo Tourism"

The Somerville News: "On My Mom Showing Me that Photo of Gram and Aunt Althea in Blackface"

Open: Journal of Arts and Letters: "Hannah in Effigy"

BODY: "Said the River When I Begged for His Song"

The Blue Mountain Review: "Textile Triolet"

Love's Executive Order: "Saving Throw"

American Poetry Journal: "Winter Break" and "Augumnootooke: Ghazal"

On the Seawall: "To My Daughter at Thirteen," "Said the River When I Begged for Their Song," and "River Sapphic"

American Literary Review: "Real Life"

I am so grateful for all those who supported me while writing this book, which in some ways I've been writing my whole life, ever since the forceps yanked me out into the delivery room of Lowell General Hospital. There are more people to thank than can possibly be named here.

Love and thanks to the river, to Lowell, to all the towns along it, to all the people, the friends who sustained me, and to all of you whose stories make up the song that makes up all of us.

This book would not exist without those who helped make these poems and this project better than I could have made it on my own. They were too generous with their time and with their brilliance. No amount of thanks is enough but, nevertheless, thank you Sarah Anderson, Lee Ann Dalton, Kate Hanson Foster, Jennifer Sperry Steinorth, Maggie Dietz, LS McKee, Hananah Zaheer Bajwa, Kerrin McCadden, Catherine Staples, Caitlin Cowan, Cindy Veach, Adam Vines, Todd Hearon, Willie Perdomo, Ralph Sneeden, Brandon Courtney, Brendan Basham, Ryan Vine, Will Brewer, Malachi Black, David Moloney, Paul Marion, Dan Albergotti, Joshua Mehigan, Jon Davis, and Jason Bremiller.

Much appreciation and so much gratitude to J. Bruce Fuller and Texas Review Press for taking a chance on this book.

Thanks for the sage counsel and mentorship, Courtney Marshall and Nat Hawkins.

Thanks to the Vermont Studio Center (especially those conversations with Brendan!), to Kim Bridgford and the Poetry by the Sea Conference, and the ineffable Word Barn for helping make this book happen.

Thanks also to Phillips Exeter Academy for its beautiful students, who are my greatest teachers, especially the Kirtland House kids who ever show me the truth.

A special thanks to January O'Neil, Andre Dubus III, Ilya Kaminsky, and John Murillo for their kind words about this book.

And, of course, all of my devotion and my love and my everything for my family, for my children, Delaney and Joseph, for my wife, Emily, for Mom and Jon and Paul, for Stacey and Laura, for my mother-in-law, Nancy, for all the cousins, aunts, and uncles, and for Joe, Frank, Ray, and Ed, kicking it together somewhere on the other side.

ABOUT THE AUTHOR

Matt W. Miller is the author of the collections *The Wounded for the Water*, *Club Icarus* (winner of the 2012 Vassar Miller Poetry Prize), and *Cameo Diner*. He has published poems and essays in *Birmingham Poetry Review*, *Harvard Review*, *Narrative Magazine*, *Southwest Review*, *Massachusetts Review*, *Adroit Journal*, and *Crazyhorse*. He is the winner of *Nimrod International*'s Pablo Neruda Prize, The Poetry by the Sea Conference's Sonnet Crown Contest, *River Styx*'s Microbrew/Microfiction Prize, and *Iron Horse Review*'s Trifecta Poetry Prize. A former Wallace Stegner Fellow in Poetry at Stanford University and a Walter E. Dakin Fellow in Poetry at the Sewanee Writers' Conference, Miller teaches English at Phillips Exeter Academy. An associate editor for *32 Poems*, he lives with his family in coastal New Hampshire.